T0125293

JEWISH SUFFERING:

THE INTERPLAY OF MEDIEVAL CHRISTIAN AND JEWISH PERSPECTIVES

ROBERT CHAZAN

Lectures on Medieval Judaism at Trinity University:
Occasional Papers

General Editor: Richard Newhauser

I.   *How the Talmud Works and Why the Talmud Won*, Jacob
        Neusner (1996)

II.   *Jewish Suffering: The Interplay of Medieval Christian and
        Jewish Perspectives*, Robert Chazan (1998)

JEWISH SUFFERING:

THE INTERPLAY OF MEDIEVAL
CHRISTIAN AND JEWISH PERSPECTIVES

Robert Chazan

Lectures on Medieval Judaism
at Trinity University:
Occasional Papers, II

MEDIEVAL INSTITUTE PUBLICATIONS

WESTERN MICHIGAN UNIVERSITY

Kalamazoo, Michigan
1998

This publication was made possible by a grant from the endowment funds of the Jewish Federation of San Antonio and by generous donations from The Great American Company, Estera and Binem Cukier, Betty and Roger S. Adler, Stewart Alexander, Linda A. and David Fisher, M.D., Elie Guggenheim, Meyer D. Lifschitz, M.D., Bernard Lee Lifshutz, Valerie Ostrower, M.D. and Victor S. Ostrower, M.D., Mr. and Mrs. Stan Studer, David Grant, Ruth and Haskel Hoine, Ph.D., Susan and Philip Lisagor, Dr. and Mrs. Marshall Nathan, and an anonymous donor.

Lectures on Medieval Judaism at Trinity University
II. (1998) Robert Chazan

Copyright © 1998 by Trinity University, San Antonio, Texas. All rights reserved.

Printed and bound by CPI Group (UK) Ltd, Croydon, CR0 4YY

ISBN 1-58044-002-9

JEWISH SUFFERING:

THE INTERPLAY OF MEDIEVAL CHRISTIAN AND JEWISH PERSPECTIVES

Tragedy and suffering, stemming either from natural forces or human design, are constants of historical experience, as is the need to comprehend such tragedy and suffering. The pain of catastrophe is mitigated considerably by understanding; it is profoundly exacerbated by a sense of meaninglessness. Most national and religious traditions develop standard explanations for tragedy. Today, even in secular American society, eruptions of the forces of nature or of human malevolence are regularly accompanied by efforts at comprehension, by provision of the solace of understanding.

Tragedy and suffering, pressing enough in all societies, are especially poignant for monotheistic religious traditions. Given the monotheistic assumption of one divine power in the world, a power that is simultaneously omnipotent and beneficent, tragedy and suffering become intensely problematic. As the first of Western monotheisms, Judaism set the course for much subsequent thinking about human tragedy. The Hebrew Bible is heavily focused on this issue, and its central messages have exerted considerable influence on later Christian, Muslim, and general Western thinking.

The simplest and most consistent biblical position on calamity is the linking of human shortcoming with divine retribution. In this way, the power of the one God remains inviolate. At the same time,

1

divine beneficence is by no means compromised, since responsibility for suffering is transferred to the human partner in the divine-human dyad.

The prophets whose utterances are recorded in the Hebrew Bible were thoroughly engaged with the vagaries of human history, in particular with the rapidly changing political constellations of the Near East. Regularly, they explained painful developments in Israelite and Judean affairs by emphasizing the interplay of human sin and divine retribution. Isaiah warned of Assyrian destruction of the northern kingdom in the eighth century, and Jeremiah foretold the impending Babylonian assault on Jerusalem in the early sixth century. Thus, when catastrophe struck, first at the hands of the former and then the latter, explanation was readily available: as the prophets had warned, God had inflicted retribution for the shortcomings of his people. This scheme, besides offering the solace of comprehension, also pointed the way to amelioration. The God who had brought punishment on his errant people would be quick to accept their repentance. Returning to the ways of the Lord would rapidly reverse the pattern of suffering.

This sin-punishment scheme dominates the historical books that stretch from Deuteronomy through II Kings. Deuteronomy includes vigorous pronouncements of the sin-punishment scheme, including elaborate descriptions of the boons that fulfillment of the covenant would confer and the horrors that transgression of the covenant would entail. The sin-punishment scheme then becomes the key to understanding the vicissitudes of Israelite history, from the period of conquest of the Holy Land down through destruction of Israelite and Judean political independence during the eighth and sixth centuries.

To be sure, the sin-punishment scheme, while appealingly simple, involved inevitable complication. There could hardly be unanimity in assessment of the rectitude of human action. Thus, for example, the historical books of Samuel and Kings judge Israelite society of the north harshly, yet we have every right to suspect that such an assessment would have been strenuously contested by the inhabitants of the northern kingdom themselves. As we proceed further into the periods of Persian, Greek, and Roman domination of Palestinian and much of the rest of world Jewry, the sense of an increasingly fragmented Jewish society deepens. When we reach the period of the Maccabean revolt against Seleucid domination, the evidence for internal fissures in Palestinian Jewry is extensive. Likewise with the period of Roman rule. Happily, we are now provided with both "majority" and "minority" views of Judean history under Roman domination. The discovery of the Dead Sea community and scrolls affords us a striking "minority" perspective on developments in Judea during the last pre-Christian and first Christian centuries. The literature of the Qumran community reveals graphically, in addition, an intense perception of "us" and "them," of those Jews destined for reward and those destined for punishment. To be sure, precisely who would be saved and who condemned was viewed quite differently among those at Qumran and within the larger Jewish community of Jerusalem.

It is in the context of this fragmented Palestinian Jewry that the first of Judaism's daughter religions was born. Earliest Christianity developed within a Palestinian matrix that showed considerable internal diversity and disagreement. Emerging in a thoroughly Jewish setting, the early followers of Jesus of Nazareth absorbed totally the regnant sin-punishment paradigm. Like the Dead Sea community, this "minority" grouping evolved its own perceptions of the working of the sin-punishment paradigm, a perception that flowed from its particular sense of the covenant between God and his chosen people.

We lack any historical sources that derive directly from the earliest phase in the history of Christianity, that point in time when the followers of Jesus saw themselves as part of Palestinian Jewry and were convinced that they were the only proper interpreters of the covenant between God and the Jewish people. It seems nonetheless certain that Jesus and his early followers would have readily fit themselves into the traditional Jewish sense that projected reward for proper comprehension and fulfillment of the covenant and punishment for distorted understanding and behavior. Some of the Gospel fulminations against the Pharisees and Sadducees, while stemming from sources that postdate the splitting off of the

Christian community from its Jewish matrix, may well reflect earlier internal Jewish tensions and disputes.

With the emergence of gentile Christianity and the growing gulf that separated the Jewish and Christian communities, the conviction of Christian accession to the riches of the Jewish past and Jewish loss of that heritage replaced the earlier sense of proper and improper Jewish understanding of the covenant. The Acts of the Apostles, the New Testament book that focuses on the movement of Christianity beyond the confines of Palestinian Jewry, is emphatic in its assertion of Christian reward and Jewish punishment. Indeed, this is the note on which the entire book concludes. The closing episode in the Acts of the Apostles portrays Paul in Rome attempting to attract Jews of that city to the Christian vision. According to the author, "some were won over by his arguments; others remained skeptical." Before the group of Jews dispersed, Paul made a final statement to them:

> How well the Holy Spirit spoke to your father through the prophet Isaiah when he said: "Go to this people and say: 'You may hear and hear but you will not understand; you may look and look, but you will never see. For this people's mind has become gross; their ears are dulled, and their eyes are closed. Otherwise, their eyes might see, their ears hear, and their mind understand, and then they might turn again and I would heal them.'"[1]

This is vigorous condemnation of Paul's Jewish contemporaries, drawn from Isaiah's great vision of the divine throne room, with God seeking an emissary to his erring people. It is worth recalling the continuation of the Isaiah vision. The prophet has agreed to serve as the Lord's messenger and has received the chilling message noted by Paul, a message of divine anger so fierce that God precludes the understanding that might lead to repentance. Seemingly stunned by the intensity of this divine wrath, the prophet asks: "How long, my Lord?" How long will this dullness of mind and spirit last? The divine answer is once more harsh in the extreme.

4

Till towns lie waste without inhabitants
And houses without people,
And the ground lies waste and desolate—
For the Lord will banish the population—
And deserted places are many
In the midst of the land.[2]

Now, it is widely agreed that the Acts of the Apostles postdates the Roman-Jewish war, the defeat of the Jews, and all the pain and dislocation that defeat entailed. The Isaiah passage just cited seems to describe a situation of desolation that corresponds nicely to the Christian perception of post-70 Jewry, a perception of destruction and exile flowing from sinfulness. For Christians, this Jewish sinfulness was readily associated with rejection of the promised messiah.

Since we have cited the Acts of the Apostles, which can fairly be called the first history of the Christian Church, we might well note also the fuller and more mature multi-volume history of the Church, penned in the fourth century by Eusebius of Caesarea. It is a rich and stimulating work, drawing on a wide range of sources and addressing a broad spectrum of issues. The core objective of this multi-faceted work was "to record in writing the successions of the sacred apostles, covering the period from our Savior to ourselves." In this work, it is striking to note the extensive interest in "the fate which has beset the whole nation of the Jews from the moment of their plot against our Savior."[3] Description of the calamities that befell the Jews from the times of Jesus down through Eusebius's own day are extensive, and the rationale for inclusion of these lengthy accounts is clear: the harsh fate suffered by the Jews was projected as sure evidence of the workings of providence in history, with the conviction that it was Jewish sinfulness, again specifically rejection of the promised messiah, that set the cycle of persecution and suffering in motion.

Even without the pressure of Christian understanding of the destruction of Jerusalem and its Temple at the hands of the Romans, Jews would have had to grapple with the impact of this massive tragedy. Simplistic invocation of the sin-punishment paradigm was fraught with difficulty, even without the additional challenge posed by Christian interpretation of the cataclysmic event. The Judaism of the Pharisees that seems to have won over the majority of Jews at the time of the conflict with Rome remained in force after the debacle; indeed, it was, if anything, strengthened by elimination of the Temple and its ritual. Post-70 Pharisaic-rabbinic leadership was hardly prepared to castigate its pre-70 predecessors as failing in religious devotion. As a result, there was no clear-cut or innovative theological explanation advanced for the Roman calamity. God remained an omnipotent and just force; his decrees always involved a measure of inscrutability. The fault surely lay with his people, although precisely how was not altogether clear. Repentance remained the key to a reversal of fortunes.

Sources for Jewish wrestling with the catastrophe of the year 70 are limited and late. The extent to which Christian views impacted upon the post-70 Palestinian Jewish community, still the largest and strongest in the world, is unclear, but the impact seems to have been minimal. Evidence from those Jewish communities for which Christianity became an increasingly potent threat is nonexistent. We can, thus, track a Christian sense of the meaning of the events of the year 70 and, to a lesser extent, a Jewish sense of the same. We have almost no evidence from these early centuries that enables us to ascertain the interplay between the two.

✿ ✿ ✿ ✿ ✿

Through the early centuries of the Middle Ages, the bulk of world Jewry lived in the orbit of Islam, relatively immune from the pressures of Christianity in general and its reading of the trajectory of Jewish history in particular. For the Jews, this meant little concern with Christian interpretations of Jewish fate and the purported sin-punishment paradigm that the Jewish past and present revealed. To be sure, Christians continued to reflect on these matters, partially because of the small but continuous Jewish presence in the Christian world and partially because the issues associated with the Jews—their rejection of Jesus, their replacement by a gentile community of believers, and the punishment purportedly attendant upon these developments—were permanently enshrined in the early and normative sources of Christian thinking.

Beginning in the eleventh century, the vitalization and expansion of western Christendom resulted in a heightened Jewish presence in the Christian sphere. This augmented Jewish presence flowed in part from the expansion of the perimeters of western Christendom, especially through reconquest of sectors of the Spanish and Italian peninsulas. In addition, the vitality of western Christendom attracted Jewish immigrants from older centers of Jewish settlement. The enhanced Jewish presence in western Christendom magnified Christian awareness of the Jews, their history, and its meaning.

At the same time, the Jews of western Christendom found themselves in an environment that challenged them profoundly. Absorbing the Hebrew Bible as part of its own Scriptures, the western Christian world claimed to understand these sacred writings properly, charging that Jewish interpretation was fatally flawed. Indeed, for the western Christian world, the proof of Jewish error was obvious in everyday terms in the downtrodden status of the Jews, traceable directly to their rejection of Christian truth, as we have already seen. The earlier Christian sense of the catastrophe of 70 as the immediate outcome of Jewish rejection of Jesus found further reinforcement in the perception of permanent Jewish degradation, evident in the continued loss of homeland, ongoing exile, and secondary and inferior status in the societies that hosted Jews.

This sense of the Jews and their fate was intensified by a generalized triumphalism in western Christendom. As this area experienced striking growth and vitalization in all spheres of its activities, ranging from demography and economics through intellectual and spiritual realms, the societies of western Christendom came increasingly to equate success with the favor of God and failure with divine abandonment. This fairly normal human propensity was of course buttressed by the underlying sin-punishment paradigm that we have already noted in both Jewish and Christian traditions. This generalized triumphalism highlighted the contrast

7

between what was perceived as Christian growth and expansion and as Jewish stagnation and decline.

Perhaps the first great expression of both the real development of western Christendom and its increasing self-confidence was the First Crusade. Called by Pope Urban II in 1095, the crusade, in its most fundamental terms, represented an effort to liberate the holy sites of Christendom from their Muslim oppressors. By the late eleventh century, vitalized western Christendom had the material resources to undertake such a bold campaign and the spiritual resolve to envision such a Herculean undertaking.[4] While the pope himself projected a fairly restricted military endeavor, his call electrified western Christendom, inflaming a variety of groups and passions in wholly unanticipated ways. Among the victims of this unbridled exhilaration were a few of the major Jewish communities of western Germany.[5]

Only one facet of the complex story of the crusader-burgher assaults of 1096 and the remarkable Jewish responses they elicited is of interest in the present context, and that involves the sense of Jewish suffering as punishment for early and ongoing sinfulness. Those few crusader bands who attacked the Jews of western Germany were said to have done so on grounds of appropriate vengeance. Both Christian and Jewish sources agree in identifying the roots of the anti-Jewish violence in the crusader sense of Jewish culpability for the crucifixion. A few (indeed very few) crusading bands extended the call for revenge against the Muslims for their alleged desecration of the holy sites into a rationale for exacting requisite vengeance against the Jews, whose crimes were far greater than those of the Muslims. Clearly, this was not a message broadcast or sanctioned by the papal court, nor did the majority of crusader armies come to such a conclusion. Occasionally, however, popular crusading bands were moved in such a direction, extrapolating from the call to take vengeance upon the Muslims justification for revenge against the Jews, whose historic sin loomed far larger than the Muslim desecration of the holy sites.[6]

Given the traditional Christian sense of God's abandonment of the Jews and the more immediate western Christian conviction of direct divine reward and punishment, it is hardly surprising to find Christians interpreting the Jewish suffering of 1096 as irrefutable evidence of divine rejection, with the conclusion that Jews must see this reality and leave the faith community that God himself had abandoned. Two of our major Jewish sources for the events of 1096—the crusader assaults and the militant Jewish responses—show Christians, generally well disposed to their Jewish neighbors, urging such understanding upon the Jews themselves, with the obvious behavioral implication that baptism constituted the only reasonable option. It surely seems that Christians did occasionally urge such conclusions upon the Jews of 1096.

The so-called *Mainz Anonymous* is our earliest and in many ways best Jewish source for the events of 1096. Its author, who seemingly wrote his narrative shortly after the assaults themselves, was committed to portraying in considerable detail a variety of Christian behaviors and attitudes and a variety of Jewish behaviors and attitudes, as well. The result is a rich and informative account of the events, an account that moves sequentially from the arousal of the crusade in France, through the movement of French crusaders into western Germany, the coalescing of German crusading bands in the latter area, and the deadly assaults in Speyer, Worms, and Mainz. It is the fullness of the report on the last of these Jewish communities that has given the narrative its widely used designation.[7]

The *Mainz Anonymous*, in its portrayal of the second attack on Worms Jewry, the attack on those Jews who had sought refuge in the bishop's palace, adopts an informative and effective literary technique of highlighting specific incidents and individuals. In two of these vignettes, the issues of Jewish fate and its meaning are raised. The first involves the Jew Simhah *ha-cohen*. The young man was urged to convert with the following argument: "Behold, all of them [the Jews of Worms] have been killed and lie naked."[8] Now, this may well be nothing more than practical counsel, although the reference to corpses lying naked suggests divine disfavor.

The second vignette, however, introduces us beyond a doubt to disaster as a meaningful spiritual sign. This second case involves a distinguished Jewess who had been hidden outside of town by friendly Christians during both the first and second attacks on

Worms Jewry. When the violence had spent itself, these erstwhile friends approached the Jewess and urged: "Indeed, you are a distinguished lady. Know and see that God no longer wishes to save you. For the slain lie naked through the streets and there is no one to bury them. Baptize yourself."[9] Here, there can be no real question as to the argument. The slaughter of Jews and their unburied state can be taken as nothing less than a sure sign of God's abandonment of the Jewish people. The long-held Christian view here takes on additional force: the slaughter of Worms Jewry constitutes a new and immediate proof of God's abandonment of the Jews. In the face of divine rejection, therefore, the only reasonable course for this important lady was conversion, which she staunchly and fatally refused.[10]

In the *Mainz Anonymous*'s depiction of events in Mainz, we encounter an alternative example of the argument of divine rejection of the Jews. In depicting the buildup of tensions prior to the full assault on Mainz Jewry by the army of Count Emicho of Flonheim, the narrator artfully inserted two incidents intended to convey growing anxiety among the Jews of Mainz. The first of these incidents involved the passage of a band of popular crusaders among whom was a woman with her ostensibly inspired goose, a phenomenon noted and excoriated by the Christian chronicler, Albert of Aachen.[11] According to the *Mainz Anonymous*, the sense of divine favor within this popular band was displayed as the group made its way through Mainz. "She [the owner of the goose] would say to all passersby: 'Behold, this goose understands my intention to go on the crusade and wishes to go with me.'" The remarkable sight attracted a crowd, which rather quickly turned on the Jews of the town, with the following related question and assertion: "Where is your source of trust? How will you be able to be saved? Behold, these signs are accomplished for us by the crucified."[12] Christians, in other words, are supported by God; Jews clearly are not. The verbal confrontation escalated into an outbreak of violence: crusaders convinced of divine support and equally convinced of divine rejection of the Jews were ready to attack; friendly burghers were opposed to this course of action. Here, the sense of

10

divine rejection is expressed by hostile Christians and leads directly to assault.

The later and longer Hebrew narrative of the events of 1096, preserved in material stemming from the late twelfth-century Jewish community of Speyer, the so-called *Solomon bar Simson Chronicle*, bases most of its account of events in Mainz on the earlier *Mainz Anonymous*. It adds some further material, however.[13] One of its additional segments depicts the tragic fate of a group of Jewish warriors led by Kalonymous ben Meshullam. Unsuccessful in their effort to hold off Count Emicho's forces at the entrance to the archbishop's palace, Kalonymous and his band found refuge in an out-of-the-way room in the lower recesses of the palace, seemingly destined for death. Archbishop Ruthard of Mainz had promised protection to his Jews, but had deserted them in the face of Count Emicho and his formidable forces. Although he had failed to protect his Jews and had fled across the Rhine River, the archbishop did not in fact forget his protégés, sending an armed escort to accompany the small band and its leader, Kalonymous, to the other side of the Rhine and safety. Unfortunately, the safety was not all that long-lived. Soon the archbishop found himself incapable yet again of protecting his Jewish clients and friends.

At this point, the archbishop addressed his friend Kalonymous, the leader of the endangered band:

> I can no longer save you. Indeed, your God has abandoned you and no longer wishes to allow you a remnant and a residue. I no longer have the strength to save you henceforth. Now, consider what you must do, you and the band with you. Either believe in our deity or else bear the sin of your ancestors.[14]

The Jews had sinned; God had rejected them. This rejection manifested itself in the current persecution: either the Jews must come to grips with this reality and its painful implications or else they would suffer the sins of their ancestors.

Thus, the vigorous Christian environment that tended to equate success with divine approbation and the traditional Christian doctrine that viewed Jewish suffering as an irrefutable sign of

11

divine rejection combined to face the Jewish victims of the 1096 violence with the argument that their suffering was but one more index of God's intense wrath and that sensible Jews must adopt the only reasonable course of action and abandon their doomed community and faith. The Jews whom we have just now encountered — Simhah *ha-cohen* of Worms, Minna of Worms, those Mainz Jews taunted by the crusading woman and her associates, and Kalonymous of Mainz—all rejected this argument and chose to remain Jewish, in the process giving up their lives. When the violence had spent itself, the question addressed to these Jews remained. In other words, the normal human need to rationalize tragedy was much enhanced by the challenge of a Christian view that explained the catastrophe in terms that entailed conversion as its logical outcome.

The Hebrew narratives that tell the story of the events of 1096 were intended to provide requisite time-bound information, thereby guiding Jewish readers for the future and explaining a series of Jewish actions that might have seemed questionable. At the same time, these narratives were addressed to timeless questions of calamity and its meanings. This grappling with the meaning of the anti-Jewish violence had to provide support and solace for the survivors of the debacle. The task of affording requisite understanding began with significant constraints. Any explanation that highlighted Jewish shortcomings would immediately strengthen the widely perceived Christian view. Obviously, compelling rationales for the tragedy had to avoid any suggestion of Jewish sinfulness as the basis for the calamity. Within these constricted parameters, how did our Jewish narrators advance theological rationales for the events they portrayed?[15]

Since I have already cited the *Mainz Anonymous* and the *Solomon bar Simson Chronicle*, I shall focus on the explanation for the tragedy found first in the earlier of the two and then in the later. The *Mainz Anonymous* was profoundly concerned with the meaning of the tragedy. The most consistent terminology that the *Mainz Anonymous* uses in portraying the catastrophe of 1096 is that of a divine decree. The sense of a divine decree plays throughout the narrative, from beginning to end; its imagery is introduced by both the actors in the drama and the auctorial observer.

The first use of this terminology comes early on, when the author completes his description of an insouciant Rhenish reply to the anguished letter dispatched by the Jews of France. "Indeed, we were not intended to hear that a decree had been enacted and that a sword was to pierce us mortally."[16] Early in his description of the fate of Speyer Jewry, the author falls back on the notion of judgment, indicating that "the decree began from there, in order to fulfill what has been said: 'Begin with my sanctuary.'"[17] The same terminology is introduced by the narrator in his depiction of the anguish of Worms Jewry upon hearing the news from Speyer.[18] At the close of his description of the twin assaults on Worms Jewry, our author puts the notion of a divine decree in the mouths of the Jews of that town itself: "It is the decree of the King. Let us fall into the hands of the Lord, and we shall thus come and see the great light."[19] When portraying the destruction of Mainz Jewry, the *Mainz Anonymous* once again uses the notion of a divine decree in its third-person narration and in remarks attributed to the Jews of 1096 themselves.[20]

Thus, from beginning to end, the imagery of a divine decree is constant. What does this imagery suggest? I would urge that this imagery is, in and of itself, neutral. It conveys the sense of a divine decision, but leaves the basis for this decision unclear. Often, such a divine decision is predicated on sinfulness, but such is not necessarily the case. Indeed, in two of the instances we have encountered, the context is quite positive. In the use of the notion of a divine decree with respect to Speyer Jewry, that Jewish community is compared favorably to the Temple in Jerusalem. Such a comparison hardly projects a decree that emanates from Jewish sinfulness. Likewise, when the Jews of Worms themselves talk of a divine decree which will result in their vision of the great supernal light, the implication can hardly be negative. Thus, imagery of a divine decree is constant, with no directly negative overtones and an occasionally complimentary context.

More positively yet, there is one recurrent phrase and conception that plays throughout the depiction of Jewish behaviors, and

13

that is the notion of *kiddush ha-Shem*, consecration of the divine Name (in this case by martyrdom). Reference to the Jews of 1096 as sanctifying the Name of God abound throughout the narrative, once more from beginning to end. At the simplest level, Jews so intensely committed to *kiddush ha-Shem* can hardly be projected as sinful, suffering the fruits of their iniquity. Indeed, there is much more than simply the assertion of *kiddush ha-Shem*. The moving accounts of Jewish martyrdom are so contrived as to brook no suggestion that they were either halakhically incorrect or that they might have been undertaken by Jews who were culpable of some significant misdeeds or even of the misdeeds of their ancestors. The targeted reader—Jewish of course—could only come away with a sense of the breathtaking devotion and heroism of these martyrs. Any perception of possible Jewish misdeeds or shortcomings would necessarily evaporate in the face of the tales themselves.

At this point, we must note a further facet of the *Mainz Anonymous*. In addition to brilliantly plotting the events of 1096 on an immediate spatial and temporal continuum, our author similarly portrayed these same events against a larger spatial and temporal backdrop. This larger spatial backdrop moved from the Rhineland, to the Holy Land, to the celestial heights; the temporal trajectory moved from 1096, through high points of the Jewish past, into early reaches of human history, and back into the pre-creation void. Projection of the Jews of 1096 into these exalted places and times once again created a picture that could hardly be challenged as to rectitude or could hardly brook notions of sinfulness and shortcoming. Jews portrayed as recreating the Temple sacrifices with their own bodies and the bodies of their loved ones; Jews depicted as the successors of Rabbi Akiba, the mother and her seven sons, Daniel and his friends, Abraham and Isaac—such Jews could hardly be assimilated to notions of a shortcoming that required divine punishment. Jews who could be depicted as carrying out an unprecedented *akedah*—meaning the sacrifice of a loved one beyond that of the patriarch Abraham—had to be seen as virtuous in the extreme. Indeed, our relatively restrained narrator bursts out, toward the end of his narrative: "Behold, has anything like this ever happened before? For they jostled one another, saying: 'I will

14

be the first to sanctify the Name of the King of all kings.'"[21] All such portrayal of the Jews of 1096 was intended to make a case for righteousness and sanctity, a case rooted in the depiction of specific behaviors and the projection of those behaviors onto a larger and most impressive spatial and temporal canvas.

Ultimately, then, the *Mainz Anonymous* certainly rebuts any Christian notion of 1096 as a punishment for Jewish sinfulness. The case made is not theoretical; it is rooted in the reality of Jewish behaviors and the terms in which the author insists on seeing those behaviors. To be sure, the narrator acknowledges an element of uncertainty. What happened was a divine decree, with the mystery that implies. However, the Jewish behaviors of 1096 represented, from the human side, acts of incomparable heroism. From the perspective of the divine-human covenant, these behaviors represented the highest possible level of human fulfillment of the divine will. Why did God choose this generation for such suffering? The *Mainz Anonymous* offers no answer. The suffering was surely not the result of sinfulness; it involved the greatest spiritual commitment and valor in the annals of the world.

The editor of the *Solmon bar Simson Chronicle* was not well focused on the historical realities of 1096; he was a collector and interpreter of the reports of others. To be sure, collection and interpretation of materials are to be cherished, as well. Our knowledge of the events of 1096 would be much diminished without the collecting zeal of our editor. Similarly, his interpretive skills surely constituted a significant contribution to post-1096 German Jewry, as it grappled with the meaning of the calamity. Our editor spins out a fairly full scheme of explanation, a scheme intended to simultaneously counter Christian claims and provide the solace of meaning.

Key to our editor's explanatory scheme was a projection of the historic sin of the golden calf as the basis for the divine decree of 1096.[22] The focus on this historic sin achieved two purposes: it negated the Christian claim of Jewish culpability and punishment for the crucifixion, and it signaled the remarkable place that Rhineland Jewry played in the span of Jewish history. The suggestion that this particular generation of Jews should have been singled out by God

15

to bear the punishment for the sin committed at the foot of Mount Sinai, while grounded in the horror of what transpired in 1096, immediately conferred unique dignity on the sufferers. Over and above all the possible generations of Jews—the great generations of the conquerors of the Holy Land under Joshua, of David and Solomon, of those who perished in the conquest of Jerusalem by the Babylonians, of Nehemiah and Ezra, of the martyrs of the Seleucid period, of the heroes of Jewish resistance to Rome, of Rabbi Akiba and his associates, of the codification of the Mishnah, of the crystallization of the two Talmuds—God had selected the Jews of 1096 to bear the onus of expiating the sin of the golden calf. While the experience of expiation involved enormous pain, the glory of being singled out by God in such a way had to be perceived as ennobling. The Jews so chosen—in the eyes of our editor—could only have been the very worthiest of all times. After laying out the claim that the Jews of 1096 had been selected to bear the punishment for the sin of the golden calf, our editor explains this choice in the following terms: "This generation was selected before him [God] as his special portion, because they had the strength and the valor to stand in his court, to do his bidding, and to sanctify his great Name in his world."[23] The pain of 1096 as punishment for contemporary Jewish shortcomings is decisively rebutted by this view.

The essential thrust of the thinking of the editor of the *Solmon bar Simson Chronicle* is toward the future. The present calamity had its roots in the far distant Jewish past; the present shows a picture of bloodshed and pain; the meaning of the events of 1096 will be fully felt in the future. That future will involve reward, on an individual and group basis, for the heroism of the martyrs; it will likewise entail punishment for the perpetrators of the catastrophe, the crusaders and their burgher allies. Both Jewish defeat and Christian victory would give way to stunning reversal. It may well be that our editor saw in the agitation to a new crusade in the twelfth century the beginnings of such a reversal.[24] We may feel that such projections of the future represent nothing more than a weak rationalization of the present and its distress; again, however, our editor did not project this reversal in the abstract. His central message was that this ultimate reversal of the outcomes of 1096 was rooted in the inevitable divine reaction to the realities as perceived and presented by his narrative—the realities of unprecedented heroism on the part of the Jewish men, women, and children subjected to the cruelty of crusader-burgher assault in 1096.

✡ ✡ ✡ ✡ ✡

The crusader assaults of 1096 have been cited, because they give us our first in-depth look at the Christian view of Jewish suffering addressed directly to the Jews as a means of bringing them to baptism and at the Jewish responses to this Christian view. To be sure, the crusading fervor that generated the unusually dramatic Christian argumentation of 1096 dissipated swiftly. The triumphalism of 1095-1099 rapidly gave way to fuller awareness of the depth and power of the Muslim world. Especially after the unsuccessful crusading effort of the 1140's, medieval western Christendom was considerably more restrained in its conviction of divine support. Since the succeeding crusades were far better organized, there was no repetition of the massacres of 1096, thus eliminating the argument from immediate catastrophe that we have encountered.

All through the succeeding centuries of the Middle Ages, however, there are continuing signs of Christians confronting Jews directly with the argument that Jewish suffering, in less immediate and dramatic form, reflects divine rejection and with the disheartening implications of this argument. We have no real evidence of serious Christian missionizing among the Jews of western Christendom during the twelfth and early thirteenth century. We do sense, however, growing spiritual pressure brought to bear on these Jews. The first two Jewish polemical works from medieval western Christendom date from the middle of the twelfth century, suggesting intensified pressures and the need to provide Jews with an effective rebuttal to major lines of Christian argumentation. It is also striking that, in both these works, the *Milhamot ha-Shem* of Jacob ben Reuven and the *Sefer ha-Berit* of Joseph Kimhi, the authors confront extensively the Christian argument concerning Jewish suffering and exile.[25] Clearly, even without a coordinated missionizing campaign, the issue of Jewish fate was very much in the air.

By the middle of the thirteenth century, the Roman Catholic Church had embarked on a serious effort to bring Jews into the Christian fold. I have elsewhere defined this effort as involving at least the establishment of regularized channels for confronting Jews with Christian claims and the adumbration of innovative argumentation based on an understanding of the Jewish audience and its vulnerabilities. Prior to the mid thirteenth century, we find no evidence for either of these commitments. During the middle decades of the thirteenth century, both suddenly appear.[26]

The newly instituted vehicles for confronting Jews with Christian truth claims were the forced sermon and the forced debate. Both involved coercing Jews to listen to the Christian message; there was no violence committed, although there was the exercise of force. Jews complained bitterly of these innovations, but to no avail. Forced sermons and forced debates became commonplace, from the thirteenth century on, in western Christendom.

Once Jews were assembled to hear the Christian case, Church leadership knew full well that new lines of argumentation had to be developed. Time-worn citations of biblical verses, the very cornerstone of Christian thinking and hence of the Christian approach to Jews, had little chance of success, although it was recurrently essayed. In the search for new and more effective lines of argumentation, a breakthrough of sorts was introduced by a convert from Judaism to Christianity, a man who was seemingly known as Saul during his days as a Jew and who became Paul subsequent to his conversion. Joining the Dominican Order, Friar Paul became an important mid-thirteenth-century missionizer to the Jews, innovating argumentation based on rabbinic materials.[27] In effect, Friar Paul argued that the authoritative books of rabbinic literature, if read by Jews attentively and without prejudice, would show that the rabbis themselves acknowledged key Christian truths. Utilizing this style of argumentation, Friar Paul covered the spectrum of issues associated with the Christian-Jewish debate: the messianic role of Jesus of Nazareth; the special qualities of Jesus, such as virgin birth, suffering, and rising from the dead; the divinity of Jesus; the

18

annulment of Jewish law as the path to salvation. In all this innovative argumentation, there was considerable emphasis on the issue of post-70 Jewish fate, again seen as dolorous and the result of Jewish sin.

A fascinating collection of Jewish polemical materials, the *Milhemet Mizvah* of Rabbi Meir Bar Simon of Narbonne, dates from the very period of the introduction of the new missionizing argumentation. In the *Milhemet Mizvah*, we see both the most traditional of Christian claims and the beginnings of the new argumentation rooted in rabbinic texts.[28] Throughout the varied segments of the collection, the Jewish author indicates clearly his perception of the issue of Jewish fate as paramount to Christian efforts to win over Jews. Let me cite only two instances of this Jewish reflection of Christian emphasis on the ongoing exile and suffering of the Jewish people.

In the *Milhemet Mizvah*, the author includes two sermons that he preached in the synagogue of Narbonne. The first of these was his rebuttal to a missionizing sermon delivered in that same synagogue on a Sabbath morning. We note here in passing the reality of the newly instituted forced sermon. Some years ago, I used the rabbi's sermon in order to reconstruct the central lines of the Christian address. Not surprisingly, this analysis showed that Rabbi Meir bar Simon was in fact reacting to an assault on Jewish exile, suffering, and hopelessness.[29]

Equally interesting is the introduction that Rabbi Meir created for his broad assemblage of anti-Christian arguments. In order to give this lengthy collection of anti-Christian claims a minimal literary setting, he provides the following brief Christian statement, as a foil to his lengthy set of Jewish rebuttals:

> Why do you not abandon completely the faith of the Jews? For you see that they are in exile this lengthy time and day by day decline. You also see, with respect to the faith of the Christians, that they day by day increase, and their successes are great all this lengthy time. You would live among us with great honor and high status instead of your current condition of exile and degradation and humiliation and accursedness.[30]

This rather brief statement, authored for the Christian protagonist by Rabbi Meir, reveals the extent to which a mid-thirteenth-century Jew saw dolorous Jewish fate as the most potent weapon in the Christian missionizing arsenal.

Our fullest sense of the new missionizing argumentation based on rabbinic sources comes from the famous forced debate held in Barcelona in 1263. Engineered by the Dominican Order with the support of King James I of Aragon, this forced debate, clearly a missionizing endeavor, involved the Christian innovator Friar Paul Christian and one of the leading Jewish authorities of the Middle Ages, Rabbi Moses ben Nahman of Gerona.[31] Friar Paul used this coerced encounter as the vehicle for testing out his innovative style of argumentation, based on the use of rabbinic materials. The claims that Friar Paul set out to prove, on the basis of rabbinic sources, were four: (1) that the messiah has already come; (2) that the messiah was intended to be both divine and human; (3) that the messiah was intended to suffer and die; (4) that, with the advent of the messiah, Jewish law was intended to lose its force. The rabbi's detailed report on the encounter indicates that the first of these assertions was in fact paramount and that it occupied center stage throughout the give-and-take. Intimately linked to the claim that the messiah has already come was the parallel contention that, with that coming, Jewish history had lost its meaning and the Jewish people had lost their primacy, indeed their significance as bearers of the covenant.

According to the rabbi's detailed narrative account, the very first source cited by Friar Paul involved the twin issues of the advent of the messiah and the onset of Jewish degradation. According to the Hebrew report, Friar Paul began by citing Genesis 49:10: "The scepter shall not depart from Judah nor the ruler's staff from between his feet, until Shiloh comes." This is one of the hoariest of biblical proof texts, and Friar Paul indicates its usual Christological reading: the Jewish people would enjoy political power until the advent of the messiah; with that advent, Jewish political power would be lost; precisely that combination can be observed in the arrival of Jesus and the subsequent loss of Jewish independence in

20

the year 70. Since this interpretation was so well known, Rabbi Moses launched into a traditional Jewish rebuttal of this timeworn Christian reading. At this point, Friar Paul introduced his new approach. He in effect said to the rabbi: Your own rabbinic sources indicate that my reading is correct. Citing a well-known passage in the Babylonian Talmud, Friar Paul indicates that the rabbis of old understood the connection between messianic advent and Jewish political power, in the form of the Palestinian patriarch and the Babylonian exilarch. Today, i.e. in the thirteenth century, concludes Friar Paul, you Jews have neither the patriarch of old nor the exilarch of old, a sure sign that the messiah has already come.[32] In making this argument, Friar Paul simultaneously addresses the issue of messianic advent and Jewish degradation, with his indication of a total eclipse of any sort of Jewish power or power figures.

The issue of Jewish fate played throughout the entire disputation. I would like to adduce only one further indication of Rabbi Moses's sensitivity to this issue. Subsequent to the conclusion of the disputation, the rabbi of Gerona authored a number of important works. The most well-known of these follow-up writings is his brilliant narrative report on the 1263 encounter. Less well known, but highly significant, is a lengthy essay entitled *Sefer ha-Ge'ulah* (The Book of Redemption), in which Rabbi Moses examines carefully the key biblical sources having to do with redemption, rebuts Christian reading of these prooftexts, and advances an extremely audacious view of the precise date on which the messiah will come, derived from a careful and brilliant analysis of the book of Daniel. The effort poured into this treatise by the great rabbi of Gerona suggests that the assault of Friar Paul touched a nerve and that the rabbi felt a responsibility to reassure his Jewish followers on the issue of historic Jewish fate.[33]

Many more late medieval sources, Christian and Jewish, could be cited to show how intensely Christians pursued the issue of Jewish fate and how thoroughly Jews understood the significance of this line of Christian missionizing attack. I shall, however, cite only one further figure, yet another convert from Judaism turned missionizer among the Jews. Abner of Burgos was a distinguished member of the Jewish community of Burgos in the late fourteenth and early fifteenth century. For decades, he agonized over conversion and eventually left the Jewish fold, resurfacing as Alfonso of Valladolid. Like Friar Paul before him, the one-time Jew became a zealous missionizer among his former brethren. While we are ill-informed with respect to the Jewish backgrounds of earlier Jewish converts like Friar Paul, with Abner/Alfonso there can be no real doubt. He was an erudite Jew, who brought his extensive Jewish learning with him into the Christian fold. His proselytizing treatises are written in a superb Hebrew, richly spiced with biblical and talmudic citation, indeed steeped in the style of rabbinic argumentation. All this Jewish learning was enlisted in the service of the Christian missionizing endeavor.[34]

Jewish exile and suffering were central elements in the missionizing treatises of Alfonso of Valladolid. Proper explication of the book of Daniel and its messianic predictions was an obsession. In his view, Jews had for ages misread the book of Daniel to reinforce their misguided belief in a future messianic redemption. Were Jews to realize the true message of Daniel, they would have no choice but to abandon their rejected faith community.[35] Alfonso's focus on the book of Daniel, the messianic advent, and dolorous Jewish faith was hardly accidental. Clearly, those were the issues that had loomed large in his own decision to leave the Jewish fold and undergo baptism. In a poignant passage, Alfonso speaks at length of the decisive moment in his conversion process:

> I saw the poverty of the Jews, my people, from whom I am descended, who have been oppressed and broken and heavily burdened by taxes throughout their long captivity—this people that has lost its former honor and glory; and there is none to help or sustain them. One day when I had meditated much on the matter, I went to the synagogue, weeping sorely and sad at heart. And I prayed to the Lord, saying: "I beseech you, O Lord God, for compassion, that you may take note of these afflictions which beset us. Why are you so angered with your people these many days, your people and the sheep of your pasture? Why should the gentiles say: 'Where is their God?' Now, O Lord, hear my prayer and my supplication and cause the light to shine upon your desolate sanctuary and have mercy upon your people Is-

rael." After the great anxieties of my heart and all the toil I had taken upon myself, I rested and fell asleep.... In a dream, I saw the figure of a tall man who said to me: "Why do you slumber? Hearken to these words that I say to you and prepare yourself against the appointed season. I say to you that the Jews have remained so long in captivity for their folly and wickedness and because they have no teacher of righteousness through whom they may recognize the truth."[36]

This is a fitting capstone to our discussion of the Christian effort at convincing Jews by hammering away at the parlous state of Jewish life. In this instance, a learned Jew seems to indicate how thoroughly such an argument might have been, on occasion, assimilated, with the Christian contention that conversion constituted the only viable alternative lived out in fact by this particular Jew.

Obviously, the bulk of medieval Jewry rejected the solution espoused by Abner/Alfonso. How, then, did these Jews counter the aggressive and difficult Christian argument? Our analysis of post-1096 Christian argumentation concerning Jewish fate has indicated that the focus shifted from catastrophic loss of Jewish life to the grinding realities of Jewish exile and inferiority. As a result, the Jewish responses shifted as well, from the exhilarated emphasis on Jewish martyrdom we encountered in the Hebrew First-Crusade narratives to a more restrained wrestling with the broader profile of Jewish and Christian historical experience.

It is useful to begin by indicating how medieval Jews did not respond to the Christian claims based on Jewish circumstances. In my readings of medieval Jewish materials, I have encountered no suggestion that the Christian evaluation of degraded Jewish circumstances was in fact incorrect, no suggestion that Jews were not mired in exile and decline. I am of course by no means suggesting that Jews lived their everyday lives in unremitting despair; such an existence is untenable. What I am suggesting is that, in the face of Christian arguments based on the notions of Jewish exile and degradation, Jews did not attack the premise, did not argue that Jewish life was in fact considerably brighter than the Christian portrait would suggest. The core notions of exile and decline were acknowledged.

However, the combination we have regularly encountered—the assertion of Jewish decline coupled with Christian success—was by no means accepted in its totality. Jewish decline was acknowledged; Christian success was often challenged, in a variety of ways. I noted earlier the rapid dissipation of the certitudes of 1095-1099, as western Christendom became increasingly aware of the depth and power of the Muslim world. That awareness extended into the Jewish minority of western Christendom, as well, and is recurrently cited. Jewish spokesmen regularly noted signs of Christian failure. They argued, for example, that in fact Muslims outnumbered Christians worldwide, suggesting that the Christian claims of universal success were highly exaggerated. Given the centrality of crusading and the significance of the Holy Land to all three Western monotheisms, it is not surprising that Jews should have pointed to conspicuous Christian failures in that arena. The inability of western Christendom to maintain its control over the Holy Land is a recurrent theme in Jewish polemical literature, again suggesting that Christian claims of divine favor are highly inflated.[37]

This line of Jewish argumentation should be seen in its broadest context. Medieval Jews, whatever their precise orientation to the study of the human past, were in fact well acquainted with a variety of historical epochs. Their own tradition highlighted the achievements and demise of a series of great powers—Near Eastern powers such as the Assyrians, Babylonians, and Persians, and Western powers such as the Greeks and Romans. Given this broad awareness of the sweep of the past, the potential for seeing western Christendom's achievements as impressive but ultimately ephemeral was high. Again, the Jews of medieval western Christendom may have been prepared to acknowledge their own difficult circumstances; they were hardly ready to cede the gift of divine favor to their Christian adversaries.

Yet more important, medieval Jews believed that the broad sweep of history hardly admitted of independent human assessment. Ultimately, for medieval Jews as for medieval Christians,

24

any assessment of historical reality and development had to be seen within the framework of divinely revealed truth. God had favored humanity by sharing key insights as to the long-term and profoundly meaningful unfolding of history. It is only against the backdrop of divinely revealed truth that real understanding of history can be achieved. Again, from both Jewish and Christian perspectives, the predictions of the prophets served as the only valid criteria for assessing the sweep of human experience. All developments of any consequence had to be fit into the pattern that God had foretold through the agency of his appointed messengers.

For medieval Jews exposed to the pressures of their Christian environment, this meant, first of all, that Christian claims of divine favor had to be scrutinized carefully against the backdrop of prophetic teaching. Jewish spokesmen did this regularly and came to the common conclusion that the Christian assertions of divine favor were inflated, indeed erroneous. The clear, God-given signs of messianic advent had not, according to Jewish observers, been realized in the realities of the medieval Christian world.

Let me illustrate this Jewish approach, very widely documented in the polemical literature, by citing an unusually dramatic and effective formulation. I have already noted the importance of the Barcelona disputation of 1263 and of Nahmanides's brilliant narrative account of the engagement. In that account, Rabbi Moses depicts himself opening the second day of the debate with a lengthy address. He is interrupted by the Christian protagonist, Friar Paul, who purportedly asks him in a straightforward manner whether he believes that the messiah has in fact already come. This is the core of the rabbi's reply:

> No. Rather, I believe and know that he has not come. There has been no one who has claimed or concerning whom it has been claimed that he is the messiah, except for Jesus. And I cannot believe that he is the messiah. For the prophet said concerning the messiah: "He shall rule from sea to sea, from the river to the ends of the earth." Jesus, however, had no rule; indeed, during his lifetime he was pursued by his enemies and forced to flee from them. Ultimately, he fell into their hands and could not save

himself. How then could he redeem all of Israel? All the more so after his death, he had no rule. For Roman rule did not come from him. Rather, even before they believed in him, the city of Rome ruled the world. After they took on his faith, they lost much power. Now the followers of Muhammed have greater rule than the Romans.[38]

Furthermore, the prophet says that, in the times of the messiah, "no longer will they need to teach one another to know the Lord; all of them shall know me." He says: "For as the waters fill the sea, so shall the land be filled with knowledge of the Lord." He also says: "They shall beat their swords into plowshares and their spears into pruning-hooks; nation shall not take up sword against nation; they shall never again know war." However, from the days of Jesus to the present, all the world has been full of violence and robbery. Indeed, the Christians spill blood more than any other people, while at the same time they are sexually promiscuous.[39]

With respect to every critical criterion—power, decency, and peace—the medieval Christian world comes up short, fails to show the signs of messianic redemption, indeed fails to show signs of broadly impressive human achievement.

The Christians claimed a combination of Jewish decline and Christian ascendancy. The latter could be fairly readily combated. The more difficult problem was to address the negative thrust, the Christian claims of abject Jewish circumstances. Here, there were broadly two lines of Jewish reply. The first is, in a way, a quieter version of the dramatic post-1096 emphasis on Jewish martyrdom. As noted, Christian claims became less dramatic after 1096, and inevitably Jewish responses did as well. However, Jewish observers did note recurrently impressive Jewish allegiance through what they portrayed as a difficult period of pre-redemptive history. In his sermon in the synagogue of Narbonne noted earlier, Meir bar Simon emphasized the quiet heroism of Jewish allegiance and assured his auditors that God, at the time of redemption, would shower additional bounty on his Jewish followers for their unflagging faithfulness.[40]

26

Emphasis on Jewish capacity for ongoing allegiance was of course predicated on the assumption that there would eventually be a redemption. Combating the negative thrust of Christian argumentation from Jewish circumstances involved Jewish thinkers inevitably in issues of future redemption and its certainty. Much of medieval Jewish thinking on eventual redemption was colored by the polemical and missionizing backdrop that has been the focus of this paper. Jews devoid of conviction in eventual redemption would have been helpless in the face of the Christian onslaught. Jews had to continue to believe and their leaders had to foster that belief.[41] Again to cite from our earlier discussion, it is striking to note the messianic speculation that Nahmanides undertook in the wake of the Barcelona encounter. Part of that endeavor involved rebuttal of Christian claims; another part of the effort involved reassurance as to future redemption of the Jewish people. In the case of Nahmanides, the end result was an unusually forthright prediction of the precise date of the messianic advent. Failure of this precise prediction to materialize was probably the major reason for the relative lack of attention accorded this major work by the great rabbi of Gerona.[42]

To provide one further indication of the lines of Jewish argumentation as to the eventual redemption that must yet come, let me cite the *Mahazik Emunah* of Rabbi Mordechai ben Joseph of Avignon, a work written at the same time and under the same stresses as Nahmanides's *Sefer ha-Ge'ulah*. This work devotes thirteen chapters to illuminating key truths about redemption. Much of the thrust of the work is negative, an effort to combat Christian claims. At the same time, there is much positive, as well. Thus, for example, the four opening chapters are designed:

(1) to prove that three exiles were announced to Israel;

(2) to prove that it was decreed that this exile [the third and present one] be longer than the other exiles;

(3) to prove and to explain the length of [this] exile, that it is the longest of all. When their messiah appeared, Israel had not yet gone into exile; thus, it is clear that the messiah had not yet

come. Thus it has been decreed, and there is a fixed end to our exile;

(4) to prove that, because of repentance, the Creator will advance the time of redemption.[43]

There is a scheme to human history decreed by God and revealed to Israel. That scheme represents divine truth and must come to pass. In this sense, rebuttal of Christian claims thus takes on positive force: since the Christian claims are obviously incorrect, the divinely revealed truths concerning redemption have not been realized. They are, therefore, very much in force for the true people of the covenant. Jewish allegiance through the trying times of Diaspora existence can only serve to enhance the rewards which God must bestow on his remarkably loyal servants.

✿ ✿ ✿ ✿ ✿

The Jews of medieval western Christendom and—to a significant degree—their predecessors and successors in the Western world lived under considerable spiritual pressure exerted by their Christian environment, its organized Church, its popular culture, its aggressiveness. The commitment of Jews to their historic heritage was always under attack, sometimes explicitly and sometimes implicitly. The range of challenges the Christian environment posed was broad and encompassing. Of these challenges, the issue of Jewish fate was surely one of the most pressing. Jewish leadership had to constantly rally its followers and did so. Resistance to Christian assertions of superiority and affirmation of the grandeur of the Jewish past and future constituted central obligations for this Jewish leadership. Jewish awareness and rebuttal of Christian claims drawn from Jewish circumstances afford us illuminating insight into the complexities of medieval Jewish experience. For the Jews living this experience such awareness and rebuttal were critical to survival.

Notes

1. Acts of the Apostles 28:24-28. I have used the New English Bible translation.

2. Isaiah 6:11. I have used the new Jewish Publication Society translation.

3. Eusebius, *The Ecclesiastical History*, trans. Kirsopp Lake et al., 2 vols., The Loeb Classical Library (Cambridge, MA: Harvard University Press, 1926-32), 1:7.

4. The First Crusade has spawned an enormous literature and continues to fascinate scholars and laymen. Three useful overviews are Steven Runciman, *A History of the Crusades*, 3 vols. (Cambridge: Cambridge University Press, 1951-54); Hans Eberhard Mayer, *The Crusades*, trans. John Gillingham (Oxford: Oxford University Press, 1972); Jonathan Riley-Smith, *The Crusades: A Short History* (New Haven: Yale University Press, 1987).

5. I have treated the 1096 assaults and the Jewish responses at length in *European Jewry and the First Crusade* (Berkeley: University of California Press, 1987).

6. Discussion of crusader anti-Jewish thinking can be found in ibid., chap. 3. In an important study, Jonathan Riley-Smith has emphasized the centrality of vengeance in crusader anti-Jewish thinking; see "The First Crusade and the Persecution of the Jews," in *Persecution and Toleration*, ed. W. J. Sheils (Oxford: Basil Blackwell, 1984), 51-72.

7. I am currently completing a full-length study of the Hebrew First-Crusade narratives, tentatively entitled *God, Humanity, and History: The Hebrew First-Crusade Narratives*. Chap. 2 of that study is devoted to the *Mainz Anonymous*.

8. The Hebrew First-Crusade narratives were published in a fine scholarly edition by Adolf Neubauer and Moritz Stern (henceforth N&S), *Hebräische Berichte über die Judenverfolgungen während der Kreuzzüge* (Berlin: Leonhard Simion, 1892), and were reedited by Abraham Habermann (henceforth Habermann), *Sefer Gezerot Ashkenaz ve-Zarfat* (Jerusalem: Sifrei Tarshish, 1945). An English translation of all three narratives can be found in Shlomo Eidelberg (henceforth Eidelberg), *The Jews and the Crusaders*

(Madison: University of Wisconsin Press, 1977). Translations of the Mainz Anonymous and the so-called Solomon bar Simson narrative can be found as an appendix to Chazan (henceforth Chazan), *European Jewry and the First Crusade*. All translations in the present publication are my own, except when otherwise noted. This passage can be found in N&S, 50; Habermann, 97; Eidelberg, 104; Chazan, 231.

9. N&S, 50-51; Habermann, 97; Eidelberg, 105; Chazan 231-232.

10. See a similar story told of the Jew David *ha-gabbai* of Mainz: N&S, 56; Habermann, 103-104; Eidelberg, 113-114; Chazan, 241-242.

11. Albert of Aachen, *Liber Christianae expeditionis*, in *Recueil des historiens des croisades, historiens occidentaux*, 5 vols. (Paris: Imprimerie royale, 1844- 95), 4:292.

12. N&S, 51; Habermann, 98; Eidelberg, 106; Chazan, 233.

13. Chap. 4 of my *God, Humanity, and History* is devoted to the utilization of the *Mainz Anonymous* by the *Solomon bar Simson Chronicle*.

14. N&S, 15; Habermann, 41; Eidelberg, 45; Chazan, 269.

15. Throughout *God, Humanity, and History*, I stress the interplay of the timeless and time-bound objectives of the Hebrew First-Crusade narratives.

16. N&S, 47; Habermann, 93; Eidelberg, 100; Chazan, 226.

17. N&S, 48; Habermann, 94; Eidelberg, 101; Chazan, 227.

18. N&S, 48; Habermann, 95; Eidelberg, 101; Chazan, 228.

19. N&S, 50; Habermann, 97; Eidelberg, 104-105; Chazan, 231.

20. Third-person references can be found in N&S, 52; Habermann, 98; Eidelberg, 106-107; Chazan, 234. First-person references can be found in N&S, 52; Habermann, 98; Eidelberg, 107; Chazan, 234.

21. N&S, 54; Habermann, 101; Eidelberg, 110; Chazan, 237-238.

22. The stance of the editor of the *Solomon bar Simson Chronicle* is developed clearly in the prologue to the work: N&S, 1-2; Habermann, 24-25; Eidelberg, 21-22; Chazan, 243-244.

23. N&S, 2; Habermann, 25; Eidelberg, 22; Chazan, 244.

24. In similar fashion, the Hebrew narrative that details Jewish circumstances during the Second Crusade, written by Ephraim ben Jacob of Bonn, may have been stimulated by the events that led up to the Third Crusade. I made such a suggestion in "R. Ephraim of Bonn's *Sefer Zechirah*," *Revue des études juives* 132 (1973), 119-126.

25. Both of these early works are available in recent scholarly editions: Jacob ben Reuven, *Milhamot ha-Shem*, ed. Judah Rosenthal (Jerusalem: Mossad Harav Kook, 1963); Joseph Kimhi, *Sefer ha-Berit*, ed. Frank Talmage (Jerusalem: Bialik Institute, 1974). The latter is also available in an English translation: Joseph Kimhi, *The Book of the Covenant*, trans. Frank Talmage (Toronto: The Pontifical Institute of Mediaeval Studies, 1972). I have discussed the former, including its concern with the onset of messianic times, in "The Christian Position in Jacob ben Reuben's *Milhamot ha-Shem*," in *From Ancient Israel to Modern Judaism: Essays in Honor of Marvin Fox*, ed. Jacob Neusner et al., 4 vols. (Atlanta: Scholars Press, 1989), 2:157-70; I have discussed the latter, with a heavy focus on the theme of Jewish suffering and messianic redemption, in "Joseph Kimhi's *Sefer ha-Berit*: Pathbreaking Medieval Jewish Apologetics," *Harvard Theological Review* 85 (1992), 417-432.

26. For a full discussion of the new missionizing endeavor, see Robert Chazan, *Daggers of Faith: Thirteenth-Century Christian Missionizing and Jewish Response* (Berkely: University of California Press, 1989).

27. For an overview of Friar Paul, see Jeremy Cohen, "The Mentality of the Medieval Jewish Apostate: Peter Alfonsi, Hermann of Cologne, and Pablo Christiani," in *Jewish Apostasy in the Modern World*, ed. Todd M. Endelman (New York: Holmes & Meier, 1987), 35-41. For Friar Paul and the innovative missionizing, see Chazan, *Daggers of Faith*, 70-85.

28. For both the traditional and innovative argumentation found in the *Milhemet Mizvah*, see ibid., 49-69.

29. See Robert Chazan, "Confrontation in the Synagogue of Narbonne: A Christian Sermon and a Jewish Reply," *The Harvard Theological Review* 67 (1974), 437-457.

30. *Shitat ha-Kadmonim 'al Massekhet Nazir*, ed. Moshe Yehudah Blau (New York: n.p., 1974), 305.

31. For full treatment of the Barcelona disputation, see Robert Chazan, *Barcelona and Beyond: The Disputation of 1263 and Its Aftermath* (Berkeley: University of California Press, 1992).

32. This argument can be found in *Kitvei Rabbenu Moshe ben Nahman*, ed. Chaim Chavel, 2 vols., 4th printing (Jerusalem: Mossad Harav Kook, 1971) 1:304-306. An English translation can be found in *Ramban: Writings and Discourses*, trans. Chaim Chavel, 2 vols. (New York: Shilo, 1978), 2:660-664.

33. The *Sefer ha-Ge'ulah* can be found in *Kitvei Rabbenu Moshe ben Nahman* 1:253-296. An English translation can be found in *Ramban: Writings and Discourses*, 2:553-650. I have treated the *Sefer ha-Ge'ulah* in *Barcelona and Beyond*, chap. 7.

34. Yitzhak Baer was vitally interested in Abner/Alfonso throughout his long scholarly career. He wrote his first essay on Abner/Alfonso in the late 1920's: "Abner aus Burgos," *Korrespondenzblatt der Akademie für die Wissenschaft des Judentums* (1929), 20-37; his fullest treatment of Abner/Alfonso can be found in the English version of his broad history of Spanish Jewry: *A History of the Jews in Christian Spain*, trans. Louis Schoffman et al., 2 vols. (Philadelphia: Jewish Publication Society of America, 1961-66), 1:327-354. For a full listing of the known writings of Alfonso and their availability in both manuscript and printed form, see Walter Mettmann, *Alfonso de Valladolid: Ofrenda de Zelos und Libro de la Ley* (Opladen: Westdeutscher Verlag, 1990), 8-9.

35. I have analyzed Alfonso's approach to the book of Daniel at some length in the proceedings of a conference held at Notre Dame University in 1994. These proceedings are scheduled for publication shortly.

36. This text was published by Isidore Loeb, "Polémistes chrétiens et juifs en France et en Espagne," *Revue des études juives* 18 (1889), 55-56. I have utilized the translation provided in Baer, *A History of the Jews in Christian Spain*, 1: 328-329.

37. This theme is, for example, prominent in the *Milhemet Mizvah*.

38. Note the introduction of the Muslims and their power into this argument.

39. *Kitvei Rabbenu Moshe ben Nahman* 1:311; an English translation can be found in *Ramban: Writings and Discourses*, 2:674-675.

40. See again Chazan, "Confrontation in the Synagogue of Narbonne."

41. The polemical thrust of much medieval Jewish eschatological speculation has not been sufficiently emphasized by previous scholarship.

42. See again Chazan, *Barcelona and Beyond*, chap. 7.

43. The Hebrew original of the chapter outline of the *Mahazik Emunah* can be found in Chazan, *Daggers of Faith*, chap. 6, n. 48; an English translation can be found in ibid., 104-106.

Robert Chazan is presently S.H. and Helen R. Scheuer Professor of Hebrew and Judaic Studies and chairman of the Skirball Department of Hebrew and Judaic Studies at New York University. He has published widely on medieval Jewish history, particularly during the First Crusade, and on Christian-Jewish relationships in the thirteenth century, the Jewish communities of Northern France, and the formation of modern anti-Semitic stereotypes. Prof. Chazan currently serves as president of the American Academy for Jewish Research and chair of the Graduate Fellowship Committee of the Wexner Foundation.

PGIL2021USA